Denver Nuggets

Michael E. Goodman

CREATIVE ✺ EDUCATION

Published by Creative Education
123 South Broad Street, Mankato, Minnesota 56001
Creative Education is an imprint of The Creative Company

Designed by Rita Marshall

Photos by: NBA Photos, UPI/Corbis Bettmann, and SportsChrome.

Photo page 1: Spencer Haywood
Photo title page: Bryant Stith

Library of Congress Cataloging-in-Publication Data

Goodman, Michael E.
Denver Nuggets / Michael E. Goodman.
p. cm. — (NBA today)
Summary: Highlights the history and key players and coaches of the
Denver Nuggets.
ISBN 0-88682-872-4

1. Denver Nuggets (Basketball team)—Juvenile literature.
[1. Denver Nuggets (Basketball team)—History. 2. Basketball—History.]
I. Title. II. Series: NBA today (Mankato, Minn.)

GV885.52.D45G66 1997   96-53024
796.323'64'0978883—dc21

First edition

5 4 3

Denver, Colorado, is one of America's most beautiful cities. It is located at the foothills of the Rocky Mountains, on a plateau a mile above sea level. Called the "Mile High City," Denver is a center of commerce, industry, and tourism. Denver has more government offices than any city outside of Washington, D.C., and half of all U.S. coins are minted in Denver.

Just before the Civil War, Denver was a small mining and cattle town, but it began to boom in the 1870s, when large deposits of gold and silver were discovered nearby. Some of

Dynamic duo Bill Hanzlik and Dan Issel.

All-Star guard Larry Jones became the first ABA player to score 50 points in a game.

the city's early residents became famous for their spirit of independence. One such person was mining tycoon Horace A.W. Tabor, who built the world-renowned Tabor Grand Opera House in Denver in 1881. At the Opera House opening, Tabor noticed a picture of William Shakespeare hanging in the lobby. "What did that man ever do for Colorado?" Tabor asked angrily. He ordered the picture removed and replaced it with his own portrait.

That same unabashed self-confidence has stayed with Denver as it has progressed into the 20th century. One source of Denver pride has been their professional basketball franchise, the Denver Nuggets. The Nuggets (nicknamed the Rockets at first) were a standout in the old American Basketball Association (ABA). They carried that success into the National Basketball Association (NBA) nine years after the franchise began.

The Nuggets have always been known for a wide-open style of offensive basketball. Some of the greatest scorers in basketball history—Spencer Haywood, Dan Issel, David Thompson, Kiki Vandeweghe, and Alex English—have entertained and amazed Denver fans over the years. Nuggets teams have achieved winning records nearly every year of the franchise's existence, and with players the likes of Bryant Stith, LaPhonso Ellis, and Antonio McDyess, they plan to carry that winning tradition into the next century.

Dan Issel, the heart of the Nuggets.

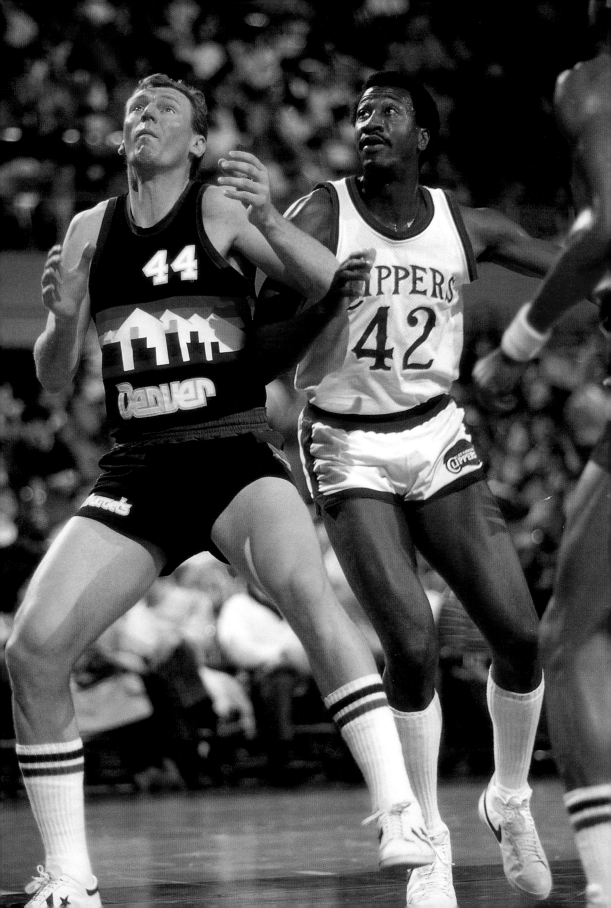

1 9 6 9

The Denver defense ranked first in the ABA under leader Wayne Hightower.

hen the ABA was formed in 1967 to challenge the established NBA, Denver was one of 10 cities chosen to
receive an ABA franchise. "At the time, we didn't really
know whether that was something to cheer about or something to be ashamed of," recalled Colorado sportscaster Jack
Stedman. No one knew whether the ABA would be able to
attract good players and coaches; they didn't know what the
level of performance might be.

Denver's first owner, James Trindle, sold the club to local
trucking executive Bill Ringsby before the team played its
first game. Ringsby also owned the Rocket Truck Lines, so
he decided to name his new team the Rockets. He even put
his company logo on the team uniforms.

The club now had a name and symbol, but no coach or
players. Denver general manager Dennis Murphy called Bob
Bass, who had coached Oklahoma Baptist College to a national small-college championship in 1966. "Murphy offered
me $20,000 to coach in Denver, which was pretty good
money, since most of the players would be making about
$8,000. So I took the job," said Bass.

"When I got to Denver, I had no players," Bass said. "We
put together a tryout camp in California. We had about a
hundred guys in the gym and it got real hot, so we opened
the doors. But it was so smoggy outside, and the smog
rolled in so thick we couldn't see and had to call off the
practice. We decided that an open tryout like that wasn't
going to do us much good, anyway. The most important

thing we did was to sign Wayne Hightower, who had played several seasons in the NBA."

Hightower was joined in Denver's 1967–68 inaugural season by a hodgepodge of unknowns, including forwards Julian Hammond and Willie Murrell, center Byron Beck, and guards Larry Jones and Willis "Lefty" Thomas. The Rockets opened the season on a positive note, whipping the Anaheim Amigos 110–105 in front of 5,000 fans in the Denver Auditorium. The club continued to play winning basketball and wound up its first campaign with a 45–33 record, third best in its division.

But the Rockets were quickly eliminated from the 1968 playoffs by the New Orleans Buccaneers. That early loss established a disturbing pattern that nearly all Denver teams have followed through the years: the club would do well during the regular season but bomb-out during the playoffs.

After another third-place finish in 1968–69, Bill Ringsby decided to take a drastic step to improve the Rockets. He offered a contract to 19-year-old Spencer Haywood, the hero of the 1968 U.S. Olympic team, who was just completing his sophomore year at the University of Detroit. Haywood—bored with the competition in college—was eager to earn money as a pro. At the time, there was an unwritten rule that pro teams would not approach college players until they had completed four years of school. But Denver, with the ABA's blessing, decided to break the rule. A furor followed, and several lawsuits were filed. In the end, Haywood was allowed to turn pro. His signing had an immediate impact on

Spencer Haywood's 2,519 points and 30-point average set league records.

Alex English, the Nuggets' all-time leading scorer.

Guard Ralph Simpson, a top scorer from an earlier era.   11

Ralph Simpson was named to the All-ABA second team during his rookie season in Denver.

pro basketball, as other outstanding college undergraduates soon followed Haywood into the ABA, including Julius Erving, George McGinnis, Ralph Simpson, and George Gervin.

Haywood had an immediate impact on the Rockets' fortunes as well. In his one season in Denver, Haywood led the ABA in both scoring and rebounding and was named Rookie of the Year and Most Valuable Player. He led the Rockets to their first Western Division crown with a 51–33 record, and helped them reach the second round of the 1970 playoffs. And by bringing crowds into the Denver Auditorium, Haywood helped the Rockets make money at a time when most ABA clubs were struggling financially.

Unfortunately for Denver fans, the Rockets' time on top was short-lived. The next season, Haywood decided to jump to the Seattle SuperSonics of the NBA. Without their star, the

Byron Beck, tough under the boards.

Rockets were a below-average club. Their record plunged to 30–54 in 1970–71, and the team fell from first to last place in its division.

CHANGING FOR THE BETTER

Dave Robisch led the Rockets in rebounding while ranking second in scoring.

Three years passed before the Rockets became a consistent winner again, and by that time a lot of changes had occurred, including the arrival of Carl Scheer in 1974 as team general manager and his hiring of Larry Brown as coach. Both Scheer and Brown came to Denver following two successful years with the Carolina Cougars.

"Bringing in Carl Scheer and Larry Brown probably saved the Denver franchise and was the reason it was strong enough to get into the NBA two years later," commented Denver center/forward Dave Robisch. "When they came to town, the Broncos [football team] owned the city, and there was serious apathy about the basketball club. We lost our first game, and nobody seemed to notice. But when we won our next nine in a row, people started packing the arena, and we became the hottest ticket in town. It was one of the fastest turnarounds in pro basketball history, from 37–47 to 65–19 in one year."

Scheer made two important changes in his first year in Denver. First, he announced that the club would move the next season to a much larger home court, the 17,000-seat McNichols Sports Arena, located just a few minutes from downtown Denver. Next, Scheer decided that the rejuvenated team also needed a new nickname. He held a contest, and the winner was "Nuggets," which had been the nickname of an earlier Denver club that had played one year in the NBA during the 1949–50 season.

Scheer and Brown put together an outstanding lineup during the 1974–75 season. The team leader was guard Mack Calvin, a great ball handler who loved to drive to the basket. Calvin was joined by Ralph Simpson in the backcourt, and Byron Beck, Dave Robisch, and rookie Bobby Jones up front. Denver had solid players and excellent coaching. The Nuggets, with their 65–19 record, achieved the finest season in ABA history.

"We were a bunch of good guys and hard workers," said Robisch, "and Larry Brown got the most out of us."

Despite their record-breaking season, the Nuggets could not overcome the Denver playoff curse. Once again, they fell short of a championship when they were eliminated by the Indiana Pacers after battling through seven tough games in the semifinals.

Scheer and Brown were determined to earn an ABA crown, and they took a major step toward that goal during the college draft in 1975. The Nuggets selected North Carolina State swingman David Thompson, a two-time College Player of the Year who was nicknamed "The Skywalker" because of his amazing leaping ability. Denver convinced Thompson to join the ABA rather than sign with the Atlanta Hawks, who had made him the first pick in the NBA draft. The young star's decision to come to Denver was a major triumph for the ABA.

"Denver had a great franchise, and I knew Carl Scheer and Larry Brown from North Carolina. So the Nuggets were a natural for me," recalled Thompson. "Atlanta wasn't in

1 9 7 5

Mack Calvin topped the league in assists and was named to the All-ABA team for a second straight year.

David Thompson, a perennial All-Star.

David Thompson was named the ABA's Rookie of the Year and All-Star Game MVP.

good shape back then. Really, it was an easy choice. It didn't matter that Denver was in the ABA, because the Nuggets were very *big league.*"

Thompson's signing made a lot more people notice the ABA, especially Denver basketball fans. After Thompson came on board, Nuggets season-ticket sales jumped from 2,000 to 6,000, and the club averaged 13,000 people per night in its new arena.

It wasn't just Thompson's phenomenal basketball skills that impressed people. He was also a warm, caring individual. "He's as great a person as he is a player," said Brown.

Thompson grew up in a small town in North Carolina, the youngest of 11 children in a deeply religious family. He liked to tell reporters that he had two homes as a child. "My father was a church deacon and my brother was a basketball nut, so you'd either find me in church or out shooting hoops," Thompson said.

By the time he finished high school, Thompson had already earned a reputation for his uncanny jumping ability. His 42-inch vertical leap, combined with his great speed and deadly accurate shooting touch, would eventually make Thompson one of the most exciting offensive players in the game. Until drug problems ruined his career in the early 1980s, Thompson was one of the greatest talents in pro basketball history.

Thompson wasn't the only new player on the Nuggets' 1975–76 roster. He was joined by forward Dan Issel, who was picked up in a trade with the Baltimore Claws, a team that folded before playing a single game. While this trade didn't attract the immediate attention of Denver fans, Issel's skills would speak for themselves over the next 10 years. When he retired in 1985, Issel was the Nuggets' all-time leader in games played, points scored, rebounds, and free throws made. He was a player who truly personified the finest qualities of the Denver Nuggets.

With Issel and Thompson, the Nuggets finished first in the ABA standings for the second straight year with a 60–24 record. Once again, they reached the ABA finals, and once again they came away without a championship. The 1976 title went to the New York Nets, led by Julius "Dr. J" Erving.

"We'll be back next year," vowed the Denver fans. But there would be no next year for the ABA.

1 9 7 7

Defensive ace Bobby Jones set club records with 186 steals and 162 blocked shots.

RIDING HIGH IN A NEW LEAGUE

By the end of the 1975–76 season, the ABA was in trouble. A number of franchises had disbanded or were going broke, attendance was generally low, and the league had been unable to land a national television contract. Still, the ABA did hold the rights to some amazingly talented basketball players, and NBA owners were interested in a merger that would bring some of the best ABA teams and players into the NBA.

Because Denver was one of the teams that had prospered in the ABA, it was accepted into the NBA merger plan, along with the New York (soon to be New Jersey) Nets, San Antonio Spurs, and Indiana Pacers. Each ABA club paid a fee of $3.2 million to enter the NBA.

In 1976–77, the Nuggets quickly proved they could be just as strong in the NBA as they had been in the ABA. Issel and

Forward Reggie Williams (pages 18–19).

WEST FARGO PUBLIC
LIBRARY

Thompson provided the best scoring tandem in the league, combining for nearly 50 points a game as the Nuggets captured first place in the Midwest Division with a 50–32 mark. Continuing the tradition, however, the Nuggets fell short in the playoffs, losing to eventual-champ Portland in the Western Conference semifinals.

The same pattern held the next season. The Nuggets topped the Midwest Division again, and this time reached the conference finals against Seattle. But the Sonics, led by former Nugget Paul Silas, were ready for Denver. Once again, the Nuggets and their fans went home dejected, without a championship.

1 9 8 0

Alex English began a 32-game streak of 40 or more points per game.

MOE MEANS "RUN, RUN, RUN"

Starting with the 1978–79 season, the Nuggets underwent a period of transition. Larry Brown decided to step down as coach in the middle of the year and was replaced by assistant Donnie Walsh, who oversaw the team's first extended losing period. Poor trades and injuries cost the Nuggets dearly. Denver was eliminated in the first round of the playoffs in 1978–79, and the next year their record fell all the way to 30–52, the second-worst mark in club history. As Thompson and Issel worked to lead the team offensively, they were joined by a third scoring sensation, Alex English, obtained in a midseason trade with Indiana.

When the team got off to another slow start in 1980–81, Walsh was fired and replaced by former Denver assistant coach Doug Moe. Moe brought a sarcastic sense of humor and a wide-open style of offense to the Nuggets. With Moe on the sidelines, Denver fans could be sure of one thing: a lot of points were going to be scored by both teams. In 1981–82, for example, the Nuggets set an all-time league scoring mark by averaging 126.5 points per game. But they also gave up a league-worst average of 126 points per game that year. And in 1983–84, the Nuggets once scored 184 points in a game—and lost. Detroit topped Denver that night, 186–184.

Kiki Vandeweghe ranked as the NBA's best outside shooter, hitting 55 percent of his field-goal attempts.

Describing Moe's coaching style in *The Official NBA Basketball Encyclopedia,* Zander Hollander wrote, "Moe had no set plays, ran short practices that were primarily conditioning drills, and told his players to shoot whenever they wanted . . . and all Moe did was win 56 percent of his games with talent that was barely above average."

Thanks to Moe's "all-offense" philosophy, the Nuggets had two players among the league's top 10 scorers each season during the early 1980s. Thompson and English were fifth and tenth in the league scoring ranks in 1980–81. In 1981–82, English and Issel were in the top 10. And in 1982–83, English and Kiki Vandeweghe, who had joined the Nuggets a year earlier, became the first teammates to rank 1–2 in scoring since the 1954–55 season. The next season, the Nuggets pair were third and fourth in the league's offensive rankings.

Not only were the Nuggets scoring tons of points during those years, they were also winning and creating a lot of excitement for Denver fans. Playing before packed houses in McNichols Arena, the club went 46–36 in 1981–82, and 45–37 in 1982–83. But the team's defensive deficiencies began to take their toll the next season, as did the club's lack

Guard Lafayette "Fat" Lever.

of a strong center or point guard to provide direction to the offense. Dan Issel was aging and just wasn't tall enough or strong enough to battle some of the league's top big men, and neither guard Rob Williams nor Mike Evans was a good floor general. Coach Moe decided that a serious rebuilding program was necessary if his team was going to keep pace in the league standings.

1 9 8 5

Under Doug Moe's run-and-gun system, the Nuggets finished 52–30, good for a conference title shot.

LEVER PROVIDES NEEDED LEADERSHIP

The rebuilding began prior to the 1984–85 season, when Denver completed a major trade with the Portland Trail Blazers. The Nuggets sent superstar Kiki Vandeweghe to Portland in exchange for three players—forward Calvin Natt, center Wayne Cooper, and guard Lafayette "Fat" Lever—and two future draft picks.

Denver fans didn't hide their displeasure with the trade. They felt that Vandeweghe's scoring skills and leadership were irreplaceable. Fortunately for the Nuggets, the fans were wrong and Moe was right. His new-look Nuggets won the 1984–85 Midwest Division title with a 52–30 record. They advanced all the way to the conference finals before being eliminated by Magic Johnson and the Los Angeles Lakers.

The players acquired in the Vandeweghe trade all made major contributions that season. Natt more than made up for Vandeweghe's absence by averaging 23.3 points and 7.8 rebounds per game, to go along with English's 28 points-per-game average. Cooper moved into the starting lineup and finished fourth in the league in shot-blocking. And Lever turned out to be the most significant acquisition of all. The

23

*Calvin Natt tied
Alex English
for the team lead
in field-goal
percentage (.504).*

razor-thin guard—nicknamed "Fat" because his younger brother couldn't say Lafayette when they were children—provided outstanding leadership. Lever directed the offense by feeding the other Denver players the ball when they were in position to score. He also joined with backcourt mate T.R. Dunn to key an aggressive new Denver defense that drove other teams crazy, forcing them into turnovers. Led by Lever, the Nuggets became a two-way threat for the first time during Doug Moe's reign.

"Fat Lever has all of these plus factors—great character, fierce competitor, best rebounding guard in the league, great defensive player, great assist man, and good scorer," said Dallas Mavericks coach Richie Adubato.

After another solid season in 1985–86 (47–35), Denver fans were thinking seriously about an NBA championship as they headed into the next season. Then the injury bug attacked the club. Calvin Natt was lost for the season with a ruptured Achilles tendon, and Wayne Cooper also suffered nagging pains. Their absence disturbed the team's delicate balance, and the club's record plunged to 37–45.

But Doug Moe wasn't about to give in. "We're going to be good," Moe assured reporters. "I promise you we'll be back."

The fiery coach turned out to be a prophet. The Nuggets rebounded in 1987–88 to win 17 more games than they had the previous year, for a division-leading 54–28 record. Alex English continued to be among the league's top scorers, while Fat Lever and newcomer Michael Adams—obtained in a trade with Washington—were among the NBA leaders in both assists and steals. Adams, a 5-foot-9 speed demon, also added a new dimension to the offense with his ability to toss in three-point field goals with amazing regularity. Adams put up 379 three-pointers during the season—more than several teams—and hit nearly 40 percent of them.

With Lever and Adams, Moe now had one of the top backcourts in the game, yet his team still had serious difficulties winning in the playoffs. The club's most glaring weaknesses were at center and power forward. As a result, the Nuggets had to rely on outscoring opponents rather than challenging them physically. That strategy could work in the regular season but became less effective during the playoffs.

Nevertheless, Doug Moe was unwilling to adapt his basic philosophy of the wide-open offensive game. Instead, he decided to change the team's personnel, and then to change his job as well.

Michael Adams's 158 three-point field goals set a new NBA record.

A NEW LOOK FOR THE 1990s

Before the 1990–91 season, a new group of owners took over the team and brought in former NBA coach Bernie Bickerstaff as general manager. Bickerstaff and Moe began an overhaul of the Nuggets that included trading the team's two veteran leaders—Alex English (who had surpassed Issel as the Nuggets' all-time scoring leader) and Fat Lever—to Dallas for draft picks that were used to acquire All-American guard Chris Jackson (who would later change his name to Mahmoud Abdul-Rauf) from Louisiana State University.

Then, in a surprising move, Doug Moe decided to step down as Nuggets coach a few months before the season began. "I'm tired of the grind of NBA coaching," the free-spirited Moe said. In his place, the Nuggets hired former

LaPhonso Ellis, a big-time rebounder (pages 26–27).

Dikembe Mutombo ranked second in the voting for NBA Rookie of the Year.

Lakers coach Paul Westhead, who had spent the past several seasons directing the nation's highest-scoring college offense at Loyola Marymount University.

Unbelievably, Westhead's offensive style was even more unstructured than Moe's had been. One writer described it as "score at all risk." When the dust finally settled, the Nuggets record was 20–62—the worst in the league. It was time for another overhaul.

The Nuggets traded their top two offensive performers of the 1990–91 season—Blair Rasmussen and Michael Adams— for high 1991 draft picks, one of which they used to pick Dikembe Mutombo, who learned his basketball under John Thompson at Georgetown. Many experts considered the 7-foot-2 native of Zaire the steal of the draft.

Over the next few years, Mutombo and Abdul-Rauf developed into two of the best players in the league. Although Denver's coaching situation turned into a game of musical chairs, behind these two standouts, the Nuggets remained competitive.

Mutombo and Abdul-Rauf led Denver to its greatest moment of the decade during the first round of the 1993–94 playoffs, when the Nuggets went up against the team with the best record in the league—the Seattle SuperSonics. The heavily favored SuperSonics won the first two games, as everyone had predicted. But with Mutombo's stellar play at center—rebounding and blocking shots—Denver won the next three games, eliminating the mighty Sonics from postseason play. Denver lost to the Utah Jazz in the next round, but during the seven-game series, Mutombo set an NBA playoff record with 38 blocks.

Over the next two seasons, Mutombo became one of the best centers in the league, and Abdul-Rauf continued to lead the team in scoring. But LaPhonso Ellis—who had also been a key part of the Nuggets' playoff victory over the Sonics—was sidelined for two years with rare injuries to both kneecaps. The Nuggets weren't sure if Ellis—who had been selected out of Notre Dame with the Nuggets' first pick in the 1992 draft—would ever be able to play again, so they acquired University of Alabama forward Antonio McDyess. McDyess had been drafted by the Los Angeles Clippers with the second pick overall in the 1995 draft. But he never wore a Clippers uniform—Denver acquired his rights on draft day.

Mahmoud Abdul-Rauf netted 93 percent of his free-throw attempts to lead the NBA.

The 6-foot-9, 240-pound McDyess was billed as a player with awesome potential. Teammate Bryant Stith compared McDyess to NBA All-Star Shawn Kemp. "Both of them are athletic, and they both came out early. You've seen the type of player Shawn has developed into. I think that Antonio has the same type of potential if he continues to work hard."

Despite the acquisition of McDyess, the club's 35–47 record in 1995–96 (the Nuggets' worst season of the decade) was enough to kill most of the optimism the club had been living on since the playoff victory over the SuperSonics. And if that wasn't enough, the Nuggets' little remaining optimism was snuffed out by the loss of Mutombo and Abdul-Rauf. Prior to the 1996–97 season, Mutombo, a free agent, signed with the Atlanta Hawks, and Abdul-Rauf was traded to the Sacramento Kings.

Veteran NBA coach Dick Motta was hired early in the 1996–97 season to run a Denver team led by McDyess and Ellis, as Mutombo and Abdul-Rauf had been replaced by

Top-shooting guard Bryant Stith.

Antonio McDyess provides muscle on the inside.

Fourth-year player Ervin Johnson had single-game career highs in rebounds (23) and blocked shots (8).

such aging and injury-prone veterans as Ricky Pierce, Dale Ellis, and Mark Jackson—players all past their prime.

The 1996–97 season was a clear indication that McDyess may need a few more years to develop into the All-Star Denver expects him to become. The season also proved that when Denver's veteran lineup stayed healthy, the Nuggets played respectable basketball and scored points behind the leadership of shooting guard Bryant Stith.

Unconvinced that the Nuggets are headed in the right direction, LaPhonso Ellis said, "I am a Nugget. I'll be a Nugget as long as I live. It just hurts me a great deal to see where we were going four or five years ago and where I dreamed I would be. And now to come back after being out for two years and see where we are—it's just sad."

But just as Ellis stated, the aging pool of veterans were no more than a finger in the dike, and that finger became less stable when both Jackson and Pierce were traded away during the season. Then coach Dick Motta and his entire staff were fired. It's clear that if the club is to become the NBA champion that Denver fans crave, they will need more players in their lineup with the drive of Ellis and the ability of McDyess—and they'll need a coaching staff that can lead the players in the right direction.